Come on, be brave.
Take a deep breath and relax.
We will enter the wonderful world of birds, to have fun coloring and learn to write some words and letters.
go ahead

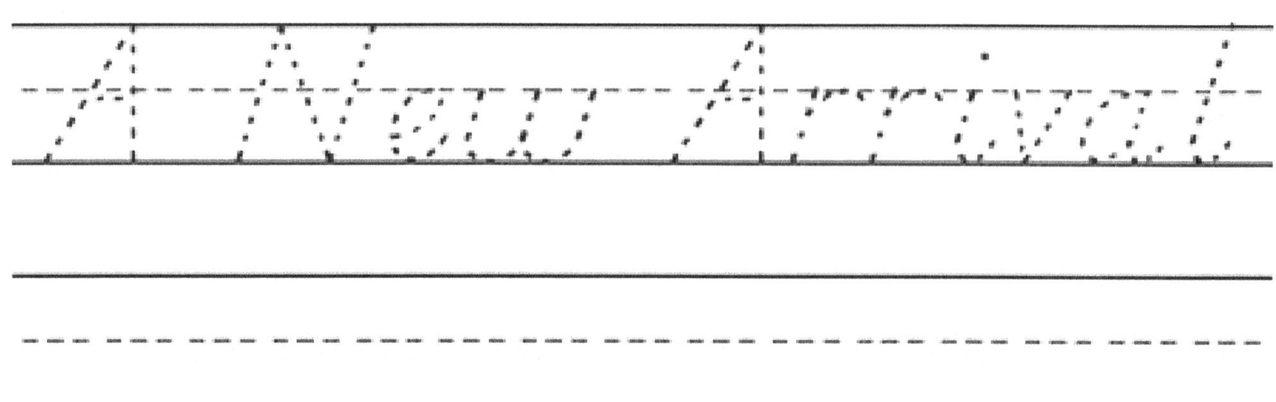
A New Arrival

B is for Bird

Baby Chick

Bird

B

BIRD

Birds

Birds in a Nest

Buzzard

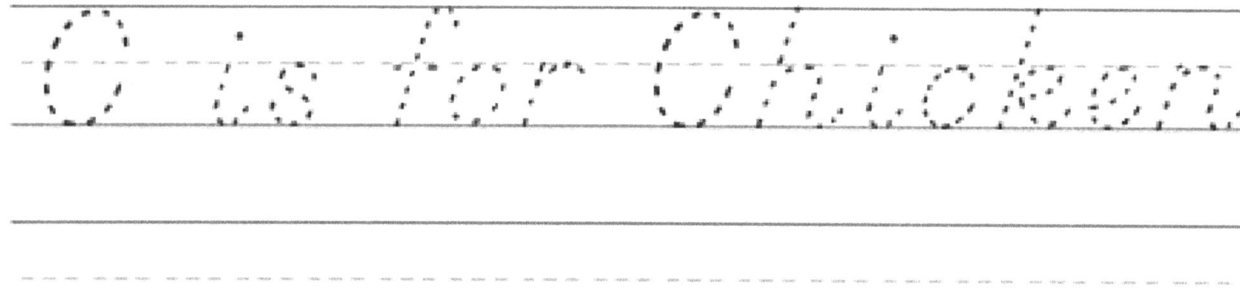
C is for Chicken.

Chick

Chicken

Chicks hatch from eggs.

Crane

D is for Duck

Dove

bird

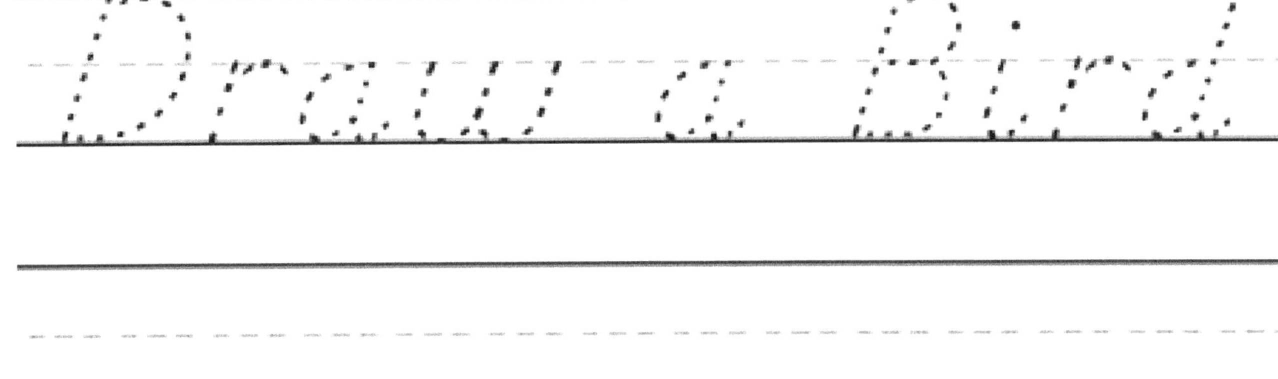

Draw a Bird

Duck

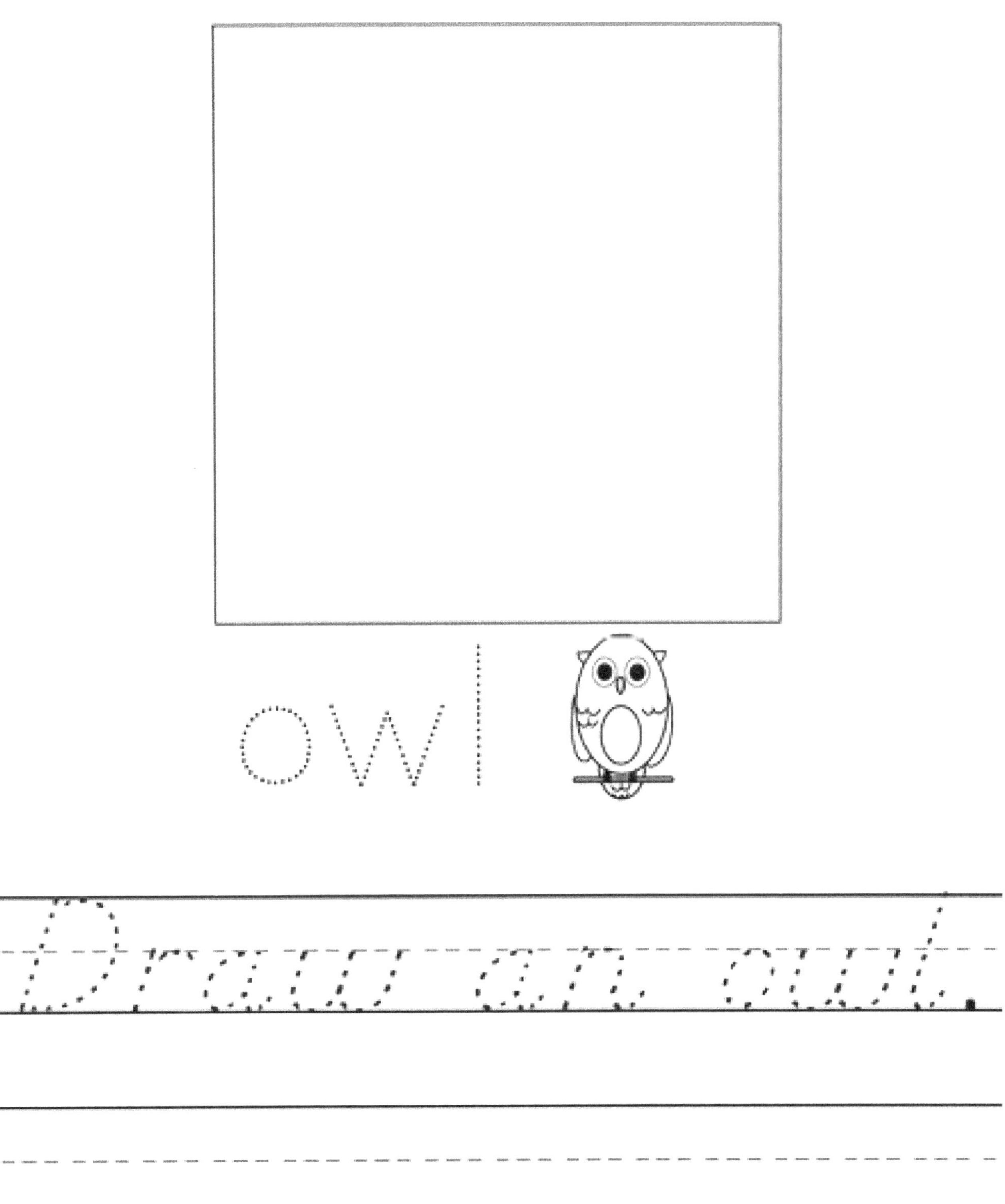

owl
Draw an owl.

Duckling

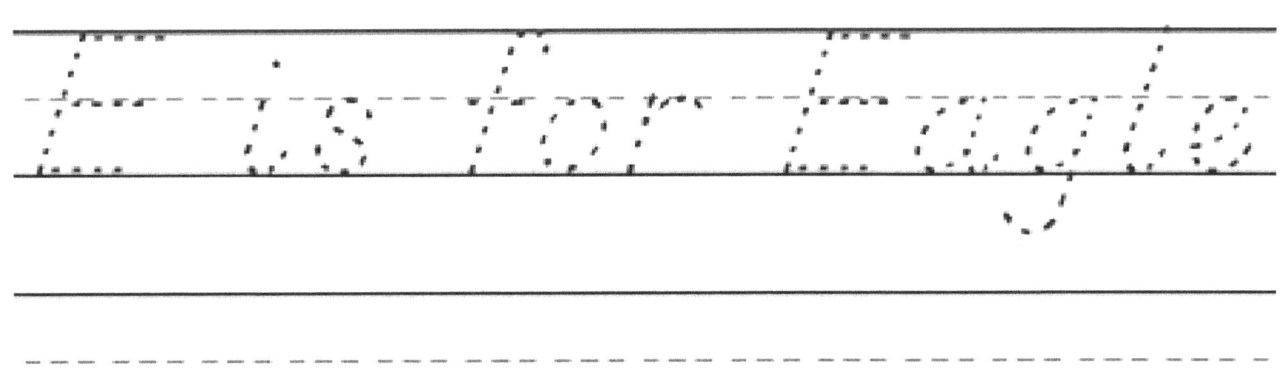
E is for Eagle

Eagle

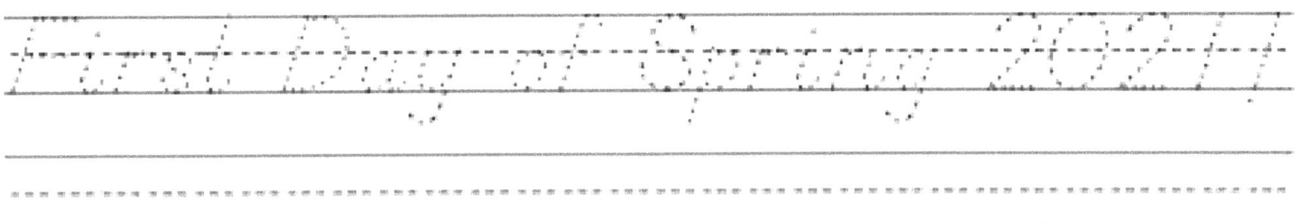
First Day of Spring 2024

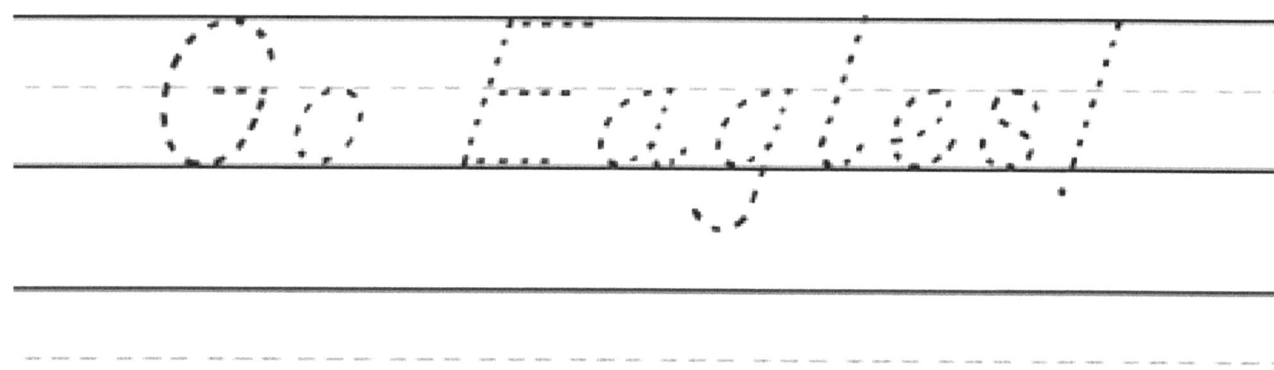

Oo Eagles!

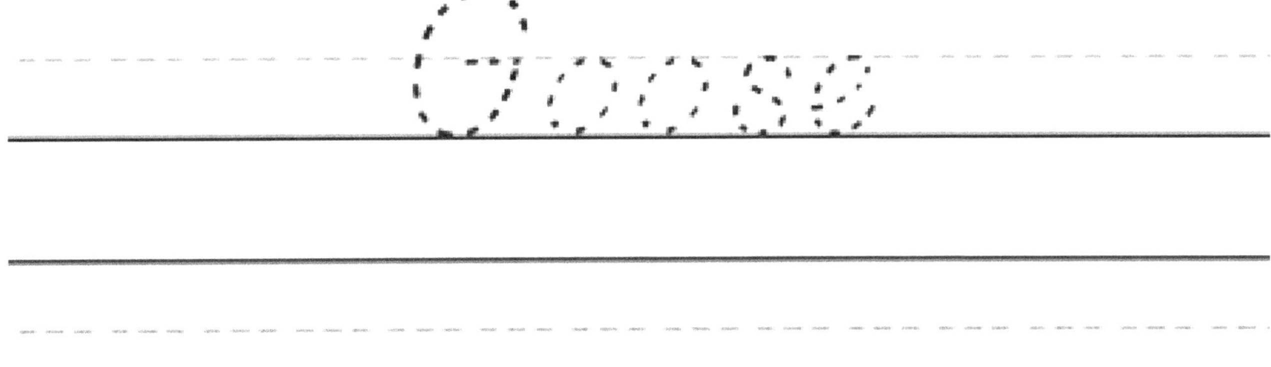
Goose

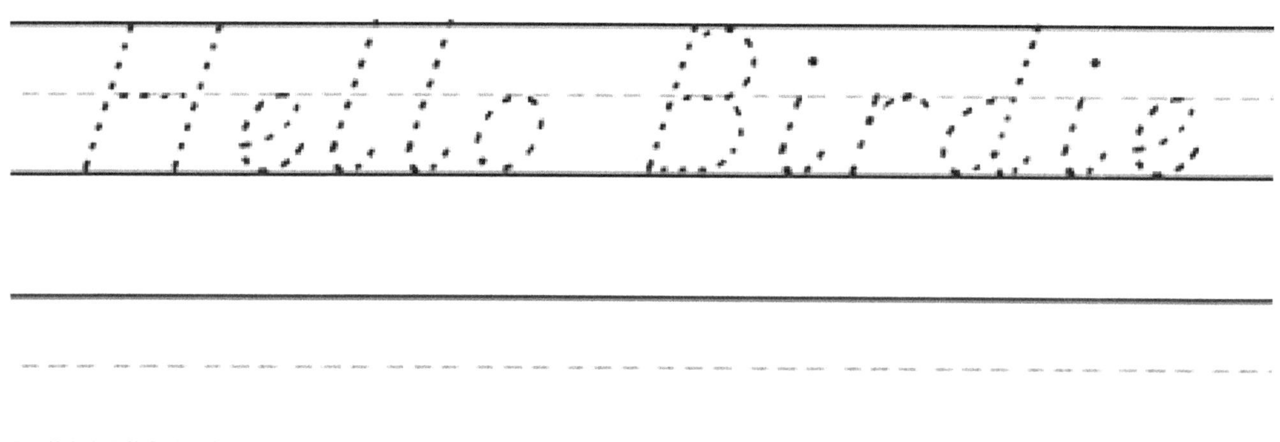
Hello Birdie

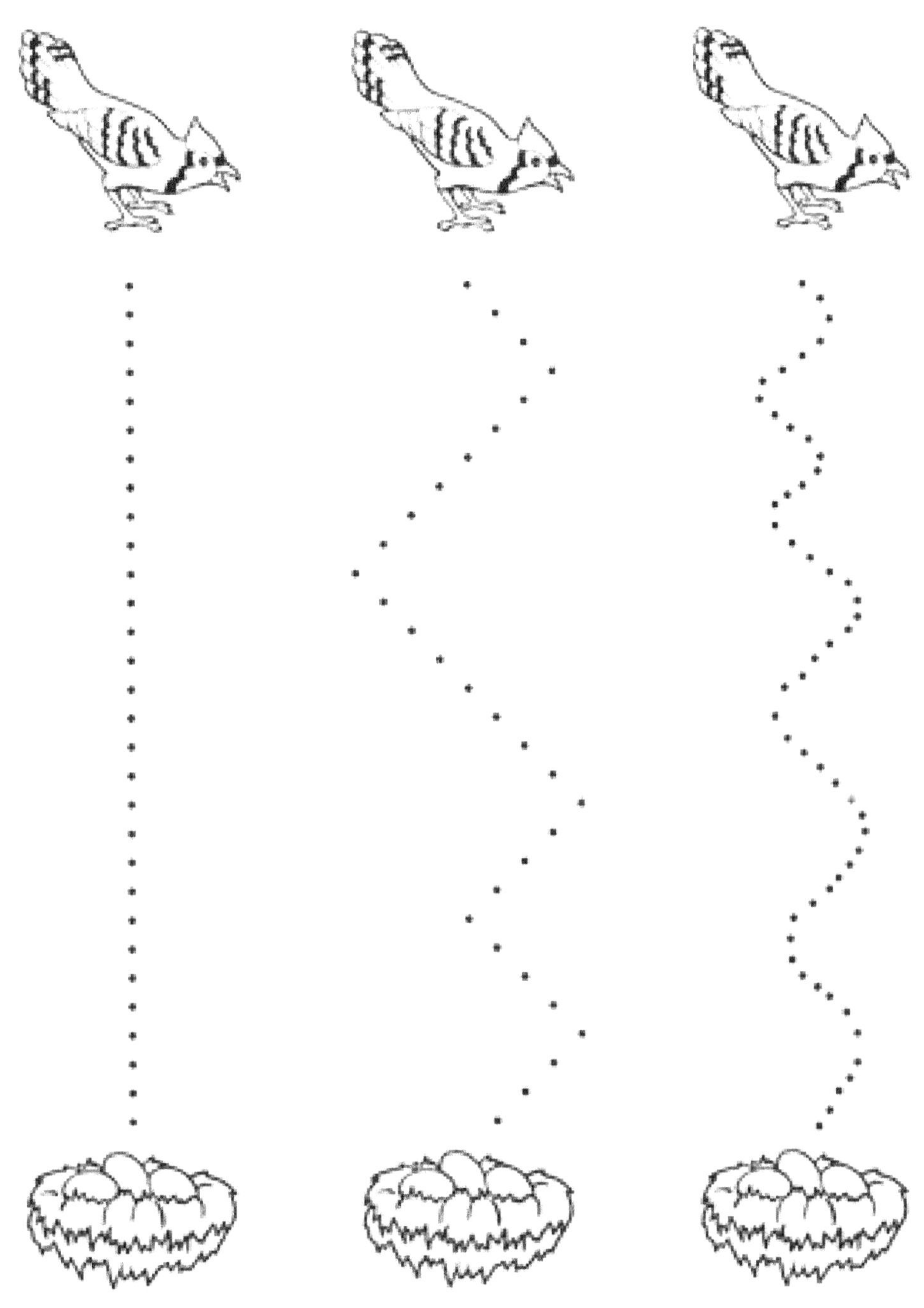

Help the bird find the nest.

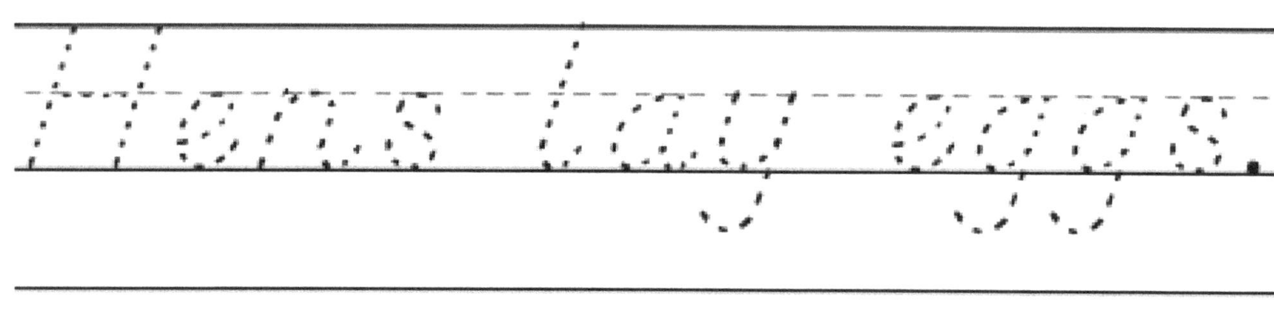
Hens lay eggs.

Hoot for Reading!

chicken

c

c

c

c

I see a chicken!

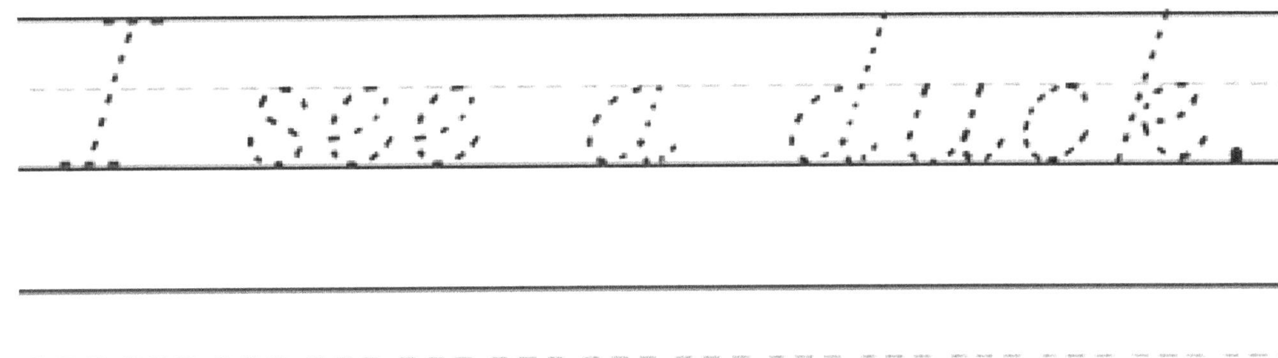

I see a duck.

Lovebirds

My Colorful Bird

My November Journal

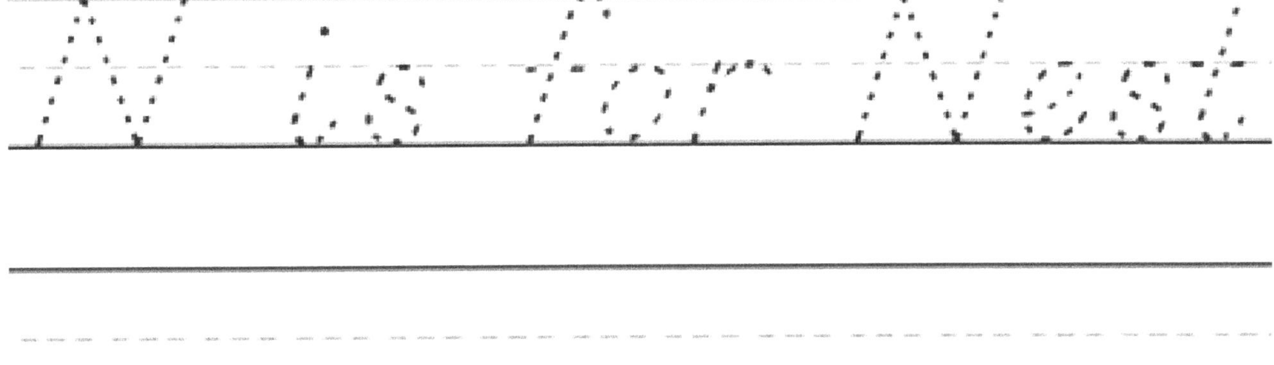

N is for Nest

Nest

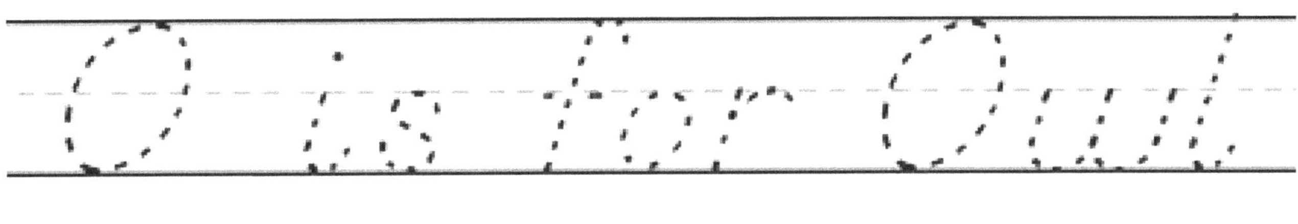
O is for Owl

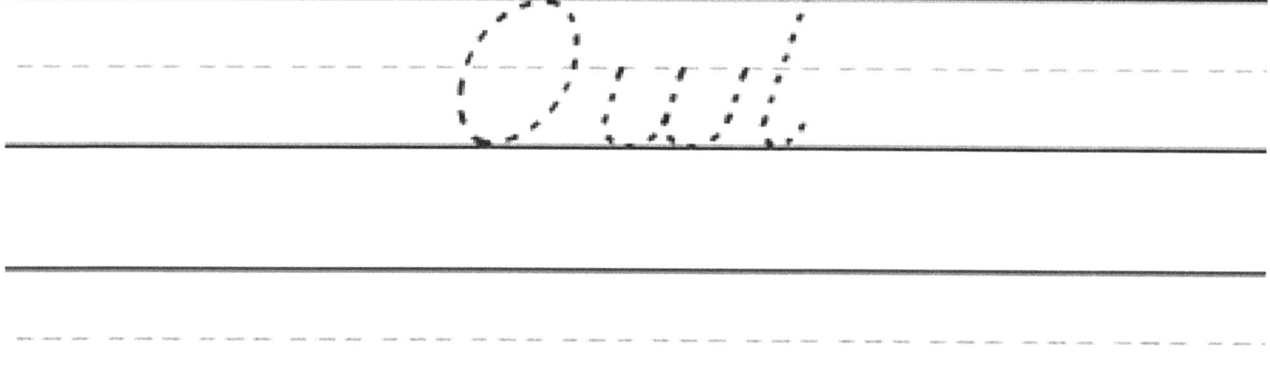

Ouri

P is for Penguin

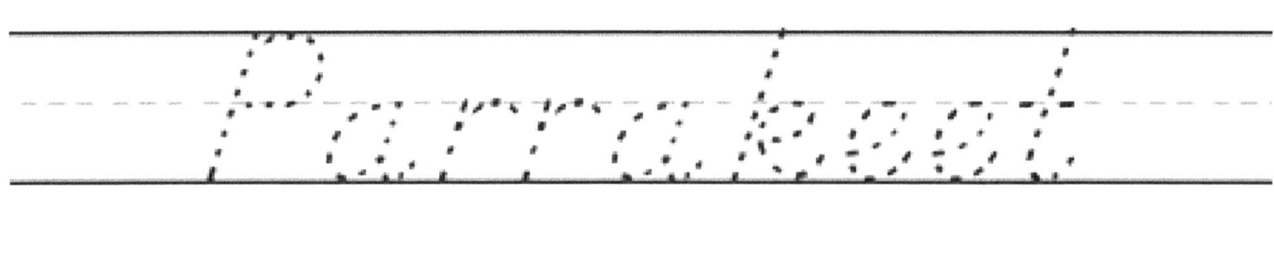
Parrakeet

Parrot

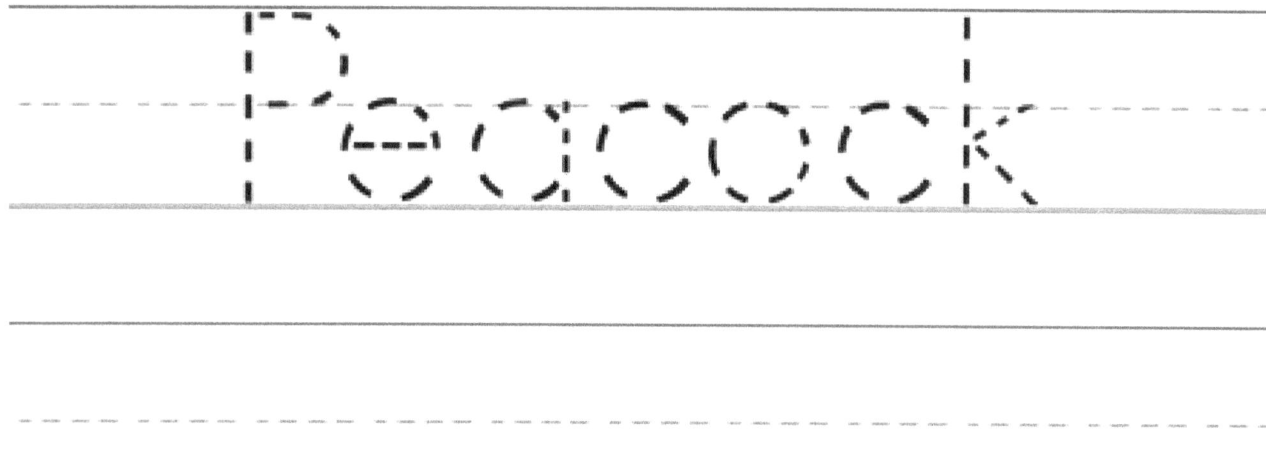
Peacock

Pellican

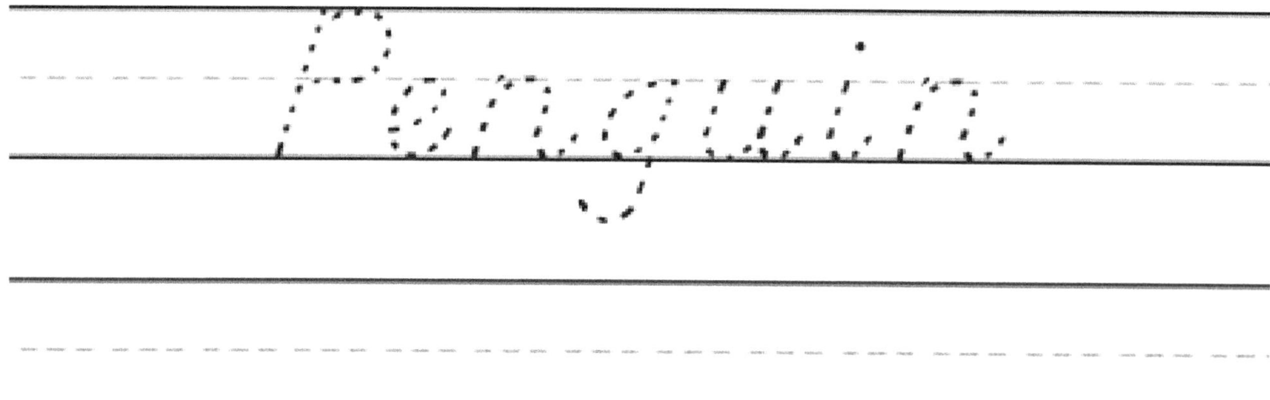
Penguin

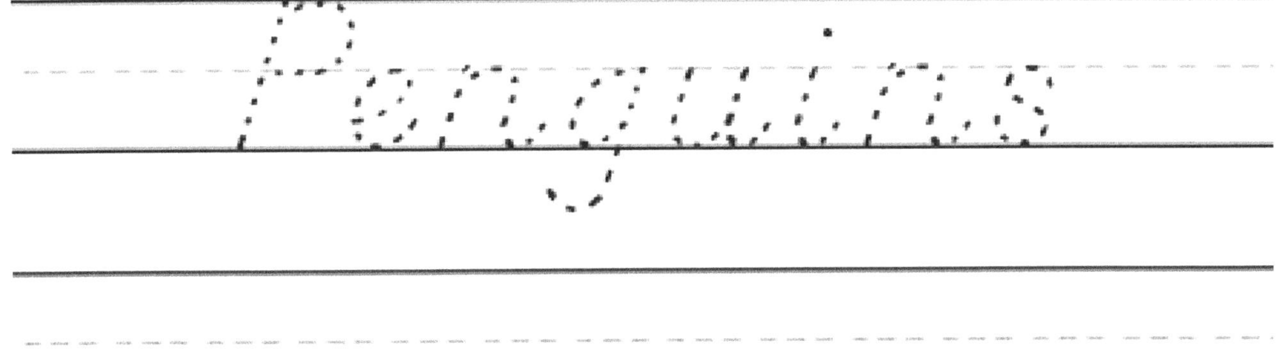
Penguins

Pink Flamingo

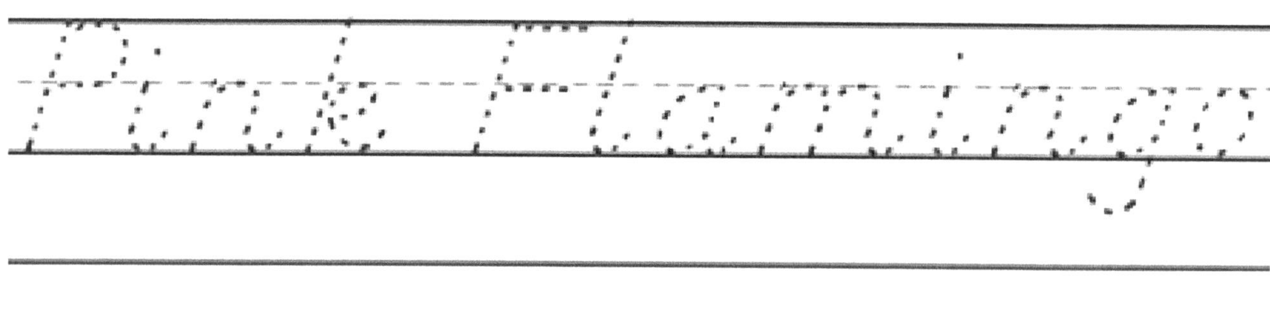

Practice writing the word bird

Quack Quack!

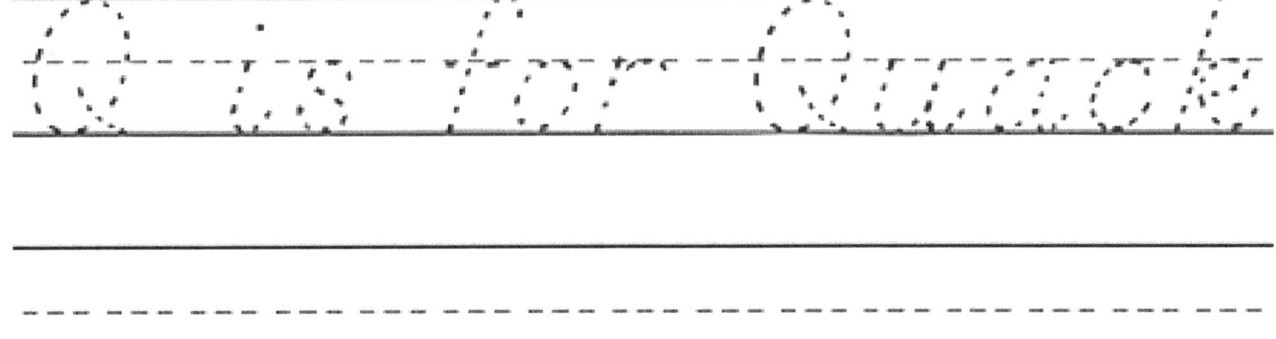
Q is for Quack

yellow duck

* 9 7 9 8 7 4 3 8 1 6 1 9 4 *